Butcher

Butcher

poems by

Natasha T. Miller

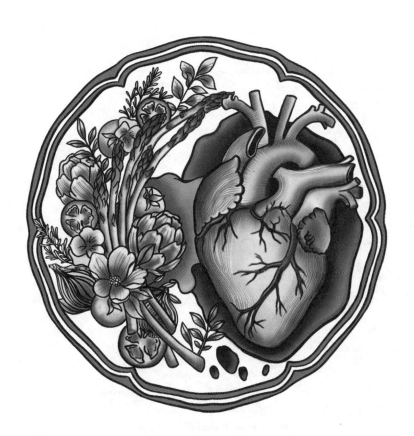

◇

Published by Button Poetry / Exploding Pinecone Press
Minneapolis, MN 55403 | http://www.buttonpoetry.com

◇

Contents

The Rib

"What Are the Consequences of Silence?" *3*

Sangria *4*

Two Fires *6*

The Answer Is Kindness *7*

Family Reunion *8*

I See You *10*

Tongue & Cheek

If I Make it Back *15*

The Other Black Man *16*

An Open Letter to Raven Symoné *18*

How to Come Out and Stay Out *20*

To Existing Being Enough *22*

The Round

Correction *25*

Ten Things You Sound Like When You Say "all lives matter" in Response to Black Lives Matter *26*

Insomnia *28*

Dear Kenneka Jenkins *29*

Nobody's Body Is a Crime *30*

Why Won't Someone Send a Tender Blue Boy to Cheer up Little Girl Blue *32*

Advice from my Grandmother *33*

The Playground Is Empty *34*

Chopped *35*

The Tenderloin

Your Son's Smile   *39*

On Turning My Nephew Into a Vegan   *40*

Frank Ocean   *41*

The Brisket

Unexpected   *45*

Grief   *46*

They Say   *47*

Say Less   *48*

Butcher   *49*

Hot Flashes   *50*

The Meaning   *52*

You Marcus   *53*

I Learned of Grief Too Late   *54*

Acknowledgments   *57*

I want to feel how I feel,
even when it's not happiness

—Toni Morrison

Butcher

The Rib

"What Are the Consequences of Silence?"

—*Mahogany L. Browne*

There's a half-empty bottle
of liquor under my mother's bed.
When I arrive at her home,

we do not speak.

I am angry.

I am silent because she's
drunk, again.

She will drink more because I refuse
to hold conversation,

I know this.

The bottle is empty by the time
I've gathered all my mail.

My throat, now
the other half of her liver,

and still, I am still
and silent.

And I swallow,
and I leave.

Sangria

My mother is fruit soaked

in alcohol. On good days I call her
sangria. The rest of the time she's

just an alcoholic. Her eyes sink
ships in a body too full of liquor to feel

itself drowning everything
that keeps it alive. Her liver,

a therapist running out of room

on the couch. One day,

the furniture will break. The house
will collapse. The bottle will finally

fall from grace. Every finger she disguised
as a petal will wilt while the rest of her

shrivels like a forgotten grape in the sun.

I will not abandon her
when her bones are too weak to walk on.

When she asks me to get her more to drink,
I will carry it to her proudly

in a paper bag, whisper, "brown
will be the color of your casket."

I will anchor every "no" in my throat

to honor the wishes of the dying
that I bring them more death.
I will tell her a story about how
a tree once spit every fruit it bore

far from its roots. I will let her die
believing that everything

skips a generation, even death.

Two Fires

We are always two fires burning
down our own home.
But not today.

Today, I choose
to be water. Today, I choose us over
the ashes.

The Answer Is Kindness

The question is my father
The answer is my mother
Buried her only son alone
Pulled holidays out of 80-hour work weeks
Feet blistering
Hands ashy
Teeth white always smiling

The question is my brother
The answer is my mother
Received the diagnosis early
Never seen him as burden
Paid for medicine out of pocket
Showed up to every hearing
Put money she didn't have on the books
Spoke highly
Never gave up on him

The question is me
The answer is my mother
A lot of addiction
A lot more surviving
A brick of confidence
A tree trunk of humility
A tiny home that survived the hurricane
The sharpest knife in any kitchen

The question is kindness
The answer is my mother
More than her demons
Heart a vending machine that cost you nothing
The most versatile cut of the cow
The rib the rib

The question kindness
The answer always my mother

Family Reunion

the day after the dead
dies it's a family reunion
the day after the dead is buried
it's a death

and you have to go to work tomorrow because
bereavement days last the same amount of time whether
you just buried your dog or
your only brother or
lost them both
and buried them right next to each other

and you have to iron your clothes now
when they can no longer see your wounds
they expect you to no longer look like shit
the obituary is already wrinkled
you start to feel like you should be
straightened out by now

it's not like he just died yesterday
it's not like people are still calling to see if you're okay

you should be able to rest now
you're not dreaming bout him anymore
because even the dead can feel when they're old news
when their sons have stopped asking
when they're coming back home

when the rest in peace shirts are too faded to remember
who you were remembering

who were you remembering?

how long has it been since their profile
became just another picture at the bottom of a police file
since their dirty clothes at the bottom of your hamper
stopped smelling like all the trouble you tried
to pray them away from

how long has it been since your friends stopped
by the house with flowers for your mother
listened to you repeat the same stories
laughed and engaged as if it was the first time they've
heard that name in years

how long has it been?

how many days does it take for a death to stop feeling
like a family reunion
for you to feel alone

like an only child
like you've lost something you love and
you can feel it now?

I See You

And if the only legacy you leave behind is stories
of your resilience
If it is only your children telling stories
about how their mother was never given a crown
but still moved like a queen

If you don't have children
and you just come from a lineage of women who sacrificed
their bellies to feed this hungry world

That is
enough

Let this poem serve as acknowledgement of your royalty

Let this poem be a reminder of how the sky would be dark
without all the days you ground your bones to powder
just to keep the lights on

Let this poem be the "Hey sis, thank you, and I see you."
when you've become invisible
to movements you've created

When you've carried sadness two times your body weight
yet still showed up to the functions smiling

When you feel less than electric
yet somehow power others with your purpose

Hey sis,
I see you

Beautiful
even when you choose not to smile

with or without makeup
in board rooms rocking skirts or pantsuits

I see you as more than feast
I see you as more than temple or structure
I see you as magic

I see you as Black girl
magic

I see you as me
too

as time's up
as our time is now

I see you in solidarity with your sisters

I see you always fighting
for others

I see you,
Sister

I see you,
Mother

I see you,
Queen

Tongue & Cheek

If I Make it Back

Today is different than
yesterday. Today I am
gay. I am out. Unsafe.
Unable to promise my mother I'll
make it home. But I am
here. Happy. Swimming in
open waters. Stroking the ocean.
Colorful. Fighting death and drowning
until the waves carry me back to shore.

The Other Black Man

when Black girls who look like Black men
                are murdered
for not succumbing to the catcalls of strangers
for not going home with men who promise their penises
                will turn us back into women
for holding our girlfriends' hands tighter
when walking past a crowd

                men looking for a fight
                looking for a dyke
                looking for a reason
to paint the cement
                we are not remembered
our deaths so unceremonious
                we die in the middle of the night
    at bus stops
                in dirty bathroom stalls
they do not march for us

                here's a joke
a woman,
a Black
and a gay
                all walk into the same bar
in the same body
                punch line

her life

        punch line

her death

        punch

her

        lying

naked in the alley

of that bar with the words "nigger" "fag" "bitch"

        burned into her skin

they don't remember us Sakia

we are not woman enough

not man enough

please, leave a record of our deaths

hang us on trees

near streetlights

give us names

just talk about us

the Black girls who look

like Black men wearing a quiet death

a sheep easy to slaughter

An Open Letter to Raven Symoné

If you tear half the label off a jar, two things happen:

1. The contents of the jar are still the contents of the jar. The label does not make it what it is, or what it is trying not to be.

2. A half-labeled jar is still a labeled jar. If you tear the part that says *peanut* off a peanut butter jar, that does not make it butter. That does not make it any less brown, or any more yellow. It does not bring it any closer to the sun. People with peanut allergies will still view it as a threat. Still shoot it down in the middle of the road in St. Louis, in a suburb in Florida. In a Wal-Mart in Ohio, on the BART in California. On a couch in Detroit. They'll say that it was playing its music so loud that they felt their throats closing. They'll kill it, blame it on an allergic reaction.

Tell me, when you went home and made love to your woman that night, did it feel like two label-less bodies, two humans free of everything except for their American, or did it feel like the Godly curves of two women, rubbing against each other, enough intensity to cum and birth a revolution? Was your pussy in her mouth? Was her breast in your hands? Did it feel like gay sex? Did it feel like this is what Brittany and Crystal in Texas died for? Not for you to only wear one of your flags. Not for you to only be gay on the internet. Not for you to try to convince Black gays that the most important thing about being Black and gay is to not be either.

Your hair might curl when it rains, but when they come for you, they will not bring water. Their guns will not be loaded with compliments for all the years you spent on Disney keeping their children company. They will not take off their hoods, lower their sickles, claim you as one of theirs. All because you don't know which country in Africa you're from. You might think that here is the only language that your skin speaks, but I can assure you that racism is one hell of a translator. Old Black or New Black, you're still Black. Outside gay or bedroom gay, you're still gay. You're still target, still one police stop or "I'm sorry I have a woman" away from your mother burying you on this same land you tried to protect. Don't make them have to remind you. You're still one of us.

How to Come Out and Stay Out

If you are out, always wear a watch.

When the unexpected hit from a pipe cracks up your skull

like the punch line of a bad Tracy Morgan joke,

look down at your wrist, know exactly what time it was

when God treated you like a joke

his bloody sense of humor has been waiting years to laugh at.

When your father's fist

leaves your face all dark and cratered,

you get up the next day

and wear the word *faggot* like an expensive pair of sunglasses.

Carry Sakia's Gunn in your mouth,

shoot back at every homophobe that tries to ruin you with words.

Bring a fruitcake to every Christmas party

that you're not really welcomed at.

Tell the kid curious about your gender

that you are not a boy or a girl;

you were born a hate crime,

an ant under a magnifying glass,

a reason to be burned.

You will be thrown off airplanes for being in love,

out of church for being yourself,

banned from sports for being open,

raped by your military to seem more American.

They will cross streets to not share a sidewalk with you,

die of thirst before drinking from a water fountain you've used,

throw cocktails through your colors.

D.L. Hughley will say, "this ain't no civil rights movement

dying over taking dick and picking cotton are not the same."

So, when you leave home

make sure your picture is exactly how you would like to be

remembered;

just in case you return as someone else or not at all.

And when the footsteps behind you start to get closer,

and the ground starts to sound like a gun range,

open your arms like your back is a bullseye

and a god is the target.

Imagine death a comedy club

you'll soon headline, each

bullet an inside joke told

just to you.

To Existing Being Enough

On days like today, you're just existing,
and that's fine.

The ocean is not always a tsunami.
The wind is not always a tornado.

You are no less powerful
in all your stillness.

The Round

Correction

America is on fire.

Correction: America is burning again.

Correction: America has always been on fire;

We are just paying closer attention to the flames.

Ten Things You Sound Like When You Say "all lives matter" in Response to Black Lives Matter

1. You invite me to a breast cancer awareness walk to honor your late auntie. I arrive wearing all red. You tell me that the colors are pink . . . and I say I know, but I don't see the point in breast cancer awareness having its own walk when people are dying of AIDS too.

2. Your family pet goes missing. You post pictures of it all around your neighborhood. I come and post pictures of other people's missing pets from around the world on top of the picture of your pet . . . well . . . because . . . you're not the only one missing a pet.

3. I show up to your grandmother's funeral and hand out my grandmothers' obituaries. You ask why. Because you ain't the only one that lost a grandma.

4. I go into a hospital and change all the intensive care unit signs to care unit signs because every life in the hospital should be cared for just the same. What makes intensive care unit patients think that their lives matter more than the life of Jenny on the first floor fighting a cold? Colds can kill too.

5. Your fiancé stands you up at the altar. As you're crying, I get up and yell millions of people get broken up with every day. Stop whining.

6. I show up at the Alcoholics Anonymous meeting to get help for my cotton candy addiction. An addict is an addict. We all deserve help.

7. You say Caylee Anthony. I say what about her, we still don't know who killed little JonBenét.

8. I say Black lives matter. You say you don't see color.

9. I say Dallas. You say blue lives matter. I say I thought you didn't see color.

10. It sounds like when I say Black lives matter, and you say all lives matter.

10. It sounds like when I say Black lives matter, you say all lives matter.

10. It sounds like when I say Black lives matter, you say all lives matter.

It sounds racist. It sounds inhumane. It sounds like you tryna choke me with my own grief. It sounds like all lives matter but when I say:

Rekia Boyd	Alton Sterling	Tamir Rice
Philando Castile	Aiyana Jones	Jessica Hernandez
Reecey Walker	Kendrick Johnson	Oscar Grant
Korryn Gaines	Michael Brown	Trayvon Martin
Nia Wilson		

You say nothing.

Insomnia

Oh America,
you sleepless
beast,
be warned that your obsession
with insomnia
and borders
will bring your own children nightmares,
not dreams.

Dear Kenneka Jenkins

It's cold for Black girls even
in the summer. It's winter for us no
matter what season it be. They'll snatch
our blood, then accuse us of not
being warm. Knowing it's not murder if
it's someone everybody already sees as
dead.

Nobody's Body Is a Crime

You are not a firearm in the hands of an unlicensed carrier
You are not twenty miles over the speed limit
not underage drinking or vandalism
neither theft nor robbery

You are not illegal

You are human

A soul connected to a source
Skin connected to bones that are weary from working ten times
harder and getting paid ninety percent less

You are your grandmother's favorite child
your lover's favorite kiss

You are in coffins in Arlington's National Cemetery

Running into burning buildings and risking your life
to save people who want you dead

The true definition of grace

Making below minimum wage barely surviving
yet still sending money back home to your family

You are a healer
a provider

Coming home every night with achy hands
tired feet and still reading your children bedtime stories
in a language that you've been hiding in your throat all day

You are more American than the American president

You are not a job or a service
or a resident or a pending status

You are not a bill being passed on the house floor in the middle of
    the night

You are flesh
You are bones
You are feelings
You are more than America's housekeepers
You are the house
You are the structure

And if you're forced to leave
you be the flames

You burn it down
You burn it down
and you write your family's name in the ashes

1.

Why Won't Someone Send a Tender Blue Boy to Cheer up Little Girl Blue

— Nina Simone

& the answer is
there are no tender blue boys
there are blue boys filled with sadness the size
of their backpacks filled with rifles for tender
blue girls who tenderly tell them no. Girls
who have not yet learned the maps of their own
bodies so reject the notion of blue boys exploring them.
& in response they end up on classroom floors in oceans
of their own blood for saying no to movie dates or not
responding to a text message. There are no tender blue
boys there are blue boys who grow into blue men who kill
their families when the now tender blue woman has
had enough. When they've been caught cheating or
when rejection on a train is enough for the blue man to
stab us to death. So please do not send the tender blue
boy to cheer up the tender blue girl because there are
no tender blue boys there are only boys that
are blue.

2.
Advice from my Grandmother

& every time a Black girl smiles, she
plans her own funeral.

She asks without showing teeth:
Am I beautiful enough to become a headline?

Can these big lips and low cheekbones make me
famous, prove my Grandmother right?

Tell her that I am in the freezer.
Cold, blood on my chin.

Still smirking, as if to say:
You've always said it'd be this mouth,
Granny, and you were right.

The Playground Is Empty

When my city turned dark & into a playground full
of ghosts, we stayed, climbed the polls, turned
the lights back on ourselves, & made so much noise
that the rest of the world had to
come back to see what was happening.

Two days after my brother died,
I peeled myself out of bed to go teach poems
to tenth graders, & a week later a girl
who had just lost her mother left a note on my desk
that only read: "thank you, thank you."

It was in that moment I understood,
success is not about money or a bottom line;
success is sometimes just the lifeline
between your journey and how your story
can inspire or save someone else.

Chopped

On this episode of Chopped
all my people make it to the dessert round.

The mandatory mystery ingredients
is shit we cooked with before.

Food ain't curated to catch us up. The judges
don't complain about the lack of salt.

They know Morton's and high blood pressure
was dropped off in our neighborhoods

to eliminate our elders from the competition early on.
So we conservative with the seasoning.

We get full access to the pantry.
The same pantry as them, as y'all.

Everybody still gets thirty minutes on the clock.

The medics come at the first sign of blood,
so we stay in the kitchen. We stay cooking, we stay cooking.

The Tenderloin

Your Son's Smile

You tryna make me believe you some type of Jesus
    Like you weren't just another Black man
With no father
    Bad habits
An untimely death
    And a sister that won't forget about you

You in Carlito's smile
    Your mama's addiction
Your father's regret
    You deserved this life as much as anyone else
You didn't start this war on drugs
    You were a casualty in it

On Turning My Nephew Into a Vegan

The hood be eating everything
even the babies

so I feed my nephew plants
try to make him smell less bloody

I hear most niggas ain't vegans

at least that's what my brother
told me before the butchers

smelled beef
slaughtered him

and left his body on the sidewalk
to cook

Frank Ocean

The day that Frank Ocean came out, not much was interrupted. Hip-hop was still hip-hop. The sun slept where the sun normally sleeps. Not much was interrupted. The day that Frank Ocean came out, my nephew sang "Thinking About You": *My eyes don't shed tears but boy they bawl when I.* Lil Wayne was thinking of the cleverest line ever about being gay to be put in a rap song. *I'm straight, no Frank Ocean.* Hip-hop was still a bloody Rubik's Cube, where grown men would rather die next to the majority than struggle to connect with their own colors. The day that Frank Ocean came out, the voice of Elmo was preparing to leave Sesame Street with a bang. Big Bird threw up in Oscar's trash can, thought about all the times he gave Elmo a ride on his back. The day that Frank Ocean came out, I let my nephew play around in heels and apply eye shadow to my lips. D.L. Hughley tweeted *seems to me sissies should be way down on the prayers list.* The day that Frank Ocean came out was a few days before his album came out. I guess hanging yourself feels better when you get to kick a pile of money and not a chair. Hip-hop was still hip hop. Lawrence King was still dead. A thirteen-year-old gay boy was somewhere tweeting his suicide letter and killing himself as a Christmas gift to his father. Two "dykes" in a Texas park were shot to death for holding hands with their lover, ignored. The day that Frank Ocean came out, my nephew was playing around in heels. I was adding his name to the prayer list, hoping that we never have to prove D.L. Hughley right. The day that Frank Ocean came out, Uganda was still Uganda preparing to pass a kill-the-gays bill and who really gave a damn? Frank Ocean gained millions of new followers; his album instantly labeled classic because of the way he used pronouns. Hip-hop was still hip-hop. Frank Ocean was out. Being gay still wasn't in, and I held my nephew tighter than ever that night. The day that Frank Ocean came out, we focused more on the mystery of his first lover than the bravery of his letter. We played it safe. We clung to Frank being bisexual. So hip-hop could still be.

The Brisket

Unexpected

I know that death is an alarm clock
without a snooze button
a morning you thought was going to give
you a few extra minutes in bed
with your lover or at the table with
your kids but instead it swept you
away without warning
took you into the unknown
without so much as
a packed bag or final goodbye

Grief

It's like opening the fridge
every few minutes hoping
that there will be food.

Except the fridge is your
heart, and the food is a
person you'll never see again.

They Say

They say you shouldn't mourn the loss of a drug dealer. Say the drug dealers stood on the tracks their whole lives. Challenging the train. Knew that even if the weather delayed it death was still. Showing up at their front door. They say the drug dealer died so casually. Say what's-his-name's-child on Joy Road or Rosa Parks Blvd., was murdered in cold blood. On his front porch. They say his. Don't say his name. Don't care about the death of a dealer. Unless he was their dealer. Gave them free drugs. Paid their rent once. Kept their lights on. Gave their kids a Christmas. They don't give the drug dealer a backstory or a reason why. He's just another one. They say he purchased the engraving so of course the bullets had his signature. They say his. Don't say his name. Say his funeral is next week. Say his funeral had a line the length of his rap sheet, curled around the corner, must've been popular. Probably could've been somebody. Don't talk about who he was. They say his casket was nice. Say his mother was nice. Was burying her only son and still. Had enough strength to stand outside the church and laugh with his niggas. They say his niggas. Don't say his name. Treat it like a weight their fragile tongues are too weak to hold. Don't wanna make the mistake of humanizing the drug dealer. Can't let anyone know they gave a damn. They say his death. I say his death. I say his in every conversation since he left. I say his grey sweats are still on a hanger in my closet. His cologne still on my dresser. I say his. It's been 1,946 days since my brother was murdered. I haven't said his name once. I say *my brother* in every conversation since his death. I say his death. I say his. I say his death. I say his. Say I'm afraid the more times I say his name. The quicker I'll empty myself of his memory. I'm scared of remembering what his name tastes like. Afraid it'll fall like ashes in my mouth. Buried underneath my tongue. My lips into a headstone. That forces me to talk about him. To stop saying his. To say his name. To say *Marcus*. To say *Marcus*. To say my brother. His name was. *Marcus*.

Say Less

My mentor told me I should find
other ways to say
"my brother"
"he died"
and "his death"

But the only words that come back to me are
My brother
He died
He's dead
His death

His death
He's dead
He died
My brother

He's dead
My brother
His death
He died

My brother's death, he died, he's dead.

Butcher

To be grace

To have the butcher turn
your chest into a cutting board

To not turn your tongue into a knife

To not cut back

To know that love is a kitchen full
of sacrifice

To be sacrificial
To be cut and not even know that you are bleeding
To say goodbye every day that you wake up on the farm

To be born livestock

To think animal better than monster

To be considered both

To arrive at the slaughterhouse still breathing

To watch the butcher prepare
to section your body off like a crime scene

To welcome the cleaver

To grin in the face of death

To taste your own blood when it splatters

To fantasize about being dinner

To hope the best cuts
make it to the table

Hot Flashes

When the oven at your mother's house goes out a day after your brother is murdered, you don't see it as a sign. You don't curse at the stove or call the electric company because you're too busy dealing with the shock of his death.

1. *When my brother was five, he burned his leg with a hot iron. Up until his cremation, the mark was so fresh on his skin that you would've thought he spent every morning trying to straighten himself out.*

2. My brother pushed me into a space heater and bent the legs on it four months before he was killed. Every day that I walked past that heater was a reminder to hold my ground and not speak to him until he apologized.

3. *The unfortunate thing about reminders is that they're rooted in the past and tend to ignore current realities; my brother died believing that I hated him.*

When the left side of the space heater goes out two days after your brother is murdered, you don't see it as a sign. You don't curse the space heater or call the manufacturer because you're too busy dealing with the shock of his death.

4. *My mother never forgave herself for leaving that iron plugged in.*

5. *You can blame anything on the dead. So it's easier to say out loud, cremation is what he would've wanted, when you're really just thinking about how much money you'll save not paying for a casket.*

Almost every night, for the first two and a half years after my brother's funeral, I would mysteriously break out into hot flashes—proof the dead can hold their grudges longer.

6. *I'll probably never forgive myself for getting my brother cremated, which confirms that I'm more like my mother than I like to admit.*

You have to confirm with the funeral home that you still choose the option to cremate, five days after your brother is murdered.

You stand outside your mother's home and ask your brother to send a sign if he doesn't want to be cremated.

A flock of birds that weren't there before all leave the rooftop and fly in the direction of the sky.

You don't see it as a sign.

You don't curse the clouds or change your mind because you're too busy frozen in the shock of his death.

The Meaning

Every time I dream about
my dead brother, I Google
the meaning of the dream

Knowing that all it's meant
in years is that he's gone.

But last night in
my dream, he broke
a mirror

and pointed to a bullet hole in
someone else's chest.

For the first time, I think,
he regrets not
being alive.

You Marcus

You Marcus
        You Martyr
        You Martyr
        You Martyr
even if you died for yourself

I Learned of Grief Too Late

I learned that grief will humble you
That there's not enough success in the world

to make you forget that your loved ones are dead

I've been an asshole to all of my friends
since my brother died

There's a girl in Detroit
that I hadn't talked to in three years
prior to the night he was murdered,

and she still showed up to the crime scene
before his body was removed from the concrete

She drank her liver into the darkest of holes and listened
to the song "Drunk in Love" with me for 56 days straight

And the first time I felt well enough
to go outside sober and sleep in the dark
alone again, I stopped answering her calls

If you're reading this, I'm sorry

Even though there's a good excuse

I know sometimes we become
the haunted and the hunter

The monster that we are running from
and the monster we are becoming

I know your phone has been ringing nonstop
Since your overdose

Since your mother passed
Since your relapse
Since your lover left
Since the very moment it happened

And you've been hitting the ignore button,
Telling yourself nobody cares about you,
I get it

Grief is more contagious than joy

It seems easier to hand our baggage
to people we love than move
through the world freely

It's the reason I left my mother
at home to mourn the death of her only
son alone while I went on the road
to perform poems for strangers

Because hurt people hurt people
is so damn cliché but true

So you blame anything on the dead

You become the excuse and the excused,
The burning building and the fire,
expecting to be rescued while left alone

Until you're left alone
and can no longer blame your behavior
on your pain

Until you have to be good to your friends again
and send apologies years too late

Until you hear someone you love say they can't forgive you
and feel success and emptiness in the same body

Until you're humbled
Until you realize that you're not the only one

We are all hurting and as a result,
all hurting each other

Until you learn to be grieving and gracious

Until you learn that this shit is never just
about you.

Acknowledgments

Thank you, Marcus, (Brother), for protecting me in life and in death. Without your life this book wouldn't be possible. Without your courage & strength my courage & strength wouldn't be possible. In death, you live on, with me, forever.

Thank you, Carlito, my beautiful, sweet, kind, tender nephew, for teaching me to say "I love you", for allowing me to help raise you and take up so much space in your life. Thank you for trusting me with so much of your life.

Thank you, Mother, for teaching me that kindness reigns supreme above all else. Thank you for giving my brother and me life. Thank you for dedicating your life to us.

Thank you, family, for always allowing me to be me without judgment, without fear, with love, and with love only.

Thank you to Detroit and my Detroit poetry family for riding with me through all of these adventures. Without your unconditional support my career wouldn't be. Whatup Doe Miles A.K.A. Mic Phelps, Tawana Honeycomb Petty, Omari, Phoenix, and so many more.

Thank you, Mahogany L. Browne, for mentorship and sisterhood. Your brilliance is all over this book and all over my career. I can't imagine I'd be here without your guidance.

Thank you, Rudy Francisco, for always being available when I need a word or a laugh. For showing me that success, grace, and kindness can all always be present.

Thank you to my friends who hear the poems first, who come to every performance, who build me up daily. It's way too many of you to name, but you know who you are.

& Thank you, Button Poetry, for believing in me and always pushing me. Thank you for giving me a platform to tell this story.

About the Author

Natasha T Miller is a Detroit, MI native, Kresge Artist Fellow, performance poet, LGBTQ activist, and film producer. Natasha has been a member of four national slam teams, starred in a national Sprite commercial, a Shinola CNN ad, and she is a Women of the World Poetry Slam three-time-top five finalist. She has awed audiences across the world at more than a hundred universities, and venues, performing in stadiums for as many as thirty thousand people. She has been in magazines such as Vogue, Elle, Entrepreneur magazine, and many more. She's had poems featured on sites like The Shaderoom, the Offing magazine, AfterEllen and many more. She opened up for the famous band Mumford and Sons in front of the first sold out crowd at Little Caesars Arena in Detroit. Natasha currently tours the world using her words to enlighten, create equality, and most importantly spread truth and forgiveness in the tradition of so many great leaders before her. When she's not performing, she's watching Food Network and thinking about what's for dinner.

Other Artist

Eboni Hogan is a Brooklyn-based poet, screenwriter and visual artist, specializing in contemporary embroidery art and illustration. Eboni is the 2010 Women of the World Poetry Slam Champion, the recipient of the 2018 Friends of Literature prize (Poetry Foundation), and a 2010 Pushcart Prize nominee. As a performance poet, she has performed in over 65 U.S. cities and internationally in Ghana, Germany and Austria. You can find more of her artwork on Instagram, @the_wreckshop.

OTHER BOOKS BY BUTTON POETRY

If you enjoyed this book, please consider checking out some of our others, below. Readers like you allow us to keep broadcasting and publishing. Thank you!

Neil Hilborn, *Our Numbered Days*
Hanif Abdurraqib, *The Crown Ain't Worth Much*
Sabrina Benaim, *Depression & Other Magic Tricks*
Rudy Francisco, *Helium*
Rachel Wiley, *Nothing Is Okay*
Neil Hilborn, *The Future*
Phil Kaye, *Date & Time*
Andrea Gibson, *Lord of the Butterflies*
Blythe Baird, *If My Body Could Speak*
Desireé Dallagiacomo, *SINK*
Dave Harris, *Patricide*
Michael Lee, *The Only Worlds We Know*
Raych Jackson, *Even the Saints Audition*
Brenna Twohy, *Swallowtail*
Porsha Olayiwola, *i shimmer sometimes, too*
Jared Singer, *Forgive Yourself These Tiny Acts of Self-Destruction*
Adam Falkner, *The Willies*
Kerrin McCadden, *Keep This To Yourself*
George Abraham, *Birthright*
Omar Holmon, *We Were All Someone Else Yesterday*
Rachel Wiley, *Fat Girl Finishing School*
Nava EtShalom, *Fortunately*
Bianca Phipps, *crown noble*
Rudy Francisco, *I'll Fly Away*

Available at buttonpoetry.com/shop and more!